CW00336995

MINCE

A collection of delicious easy-to-make recipes

Contents

All rights reserved.

No part of this publication may be reproduced, stored in a retrieval system or transmitted by any means (electronic, mechanical, photocopying or otherwise) without the prior permission of the publisher.

Originally published in 2009 by L&K Designs. This edition published for Myriad Books Limited in 2010.
© L&K Designs 2009
PRINTED IN CHINA

Publishers Disclaimer

The recipes contained in this book are passed on in good faith but the publisher cannot be held responsible for any adverse results. Please be aware that certain recipes may contain nuts.

The photographs in this book are for illustrative purposes only and do not represent the finished recipe.
Photographs © Getty Images, Jupiter Images, Image Source and Shutterstock.

Marvellous Mince

Mince, a family favourite for many years, is centre stage in this book packed with delicious easy to follow recipes.

From the classic and traditional comfort foods of Shepherd's Pie, Spaghetti Bolognese and Lasagne, through to exotic curries, zingy burgers and mouthwatering meatballs.

Including recipes for minced beef, lamb, pork and turkey the book is divided into sections for ease of use, with an index of recipes and a section for you to record your own mince recipes.

Covering the traditional and not so traditional, from delicious dinners through to after-work suppers this book will help you fall in love with mince all over again!

Minced beef (Ground beef)

The most common form of mince, used in various dishes such as hamburgers, meatballs and spaghetti sauces. Prices can vary on minced beef, depending on the cut of beef which has been minced. Steak mince for instance is now a popular choice.

Turkey Mince

This is becoming ever more popular all over the world, as it is much healthier than other minced meats. It can easily replace minced beef for recipes such as meatballs, hamburgers and tacos.

Lamb Mince

Another alternative to minced beef, lamb mince is arguably the tastiest minced meat available, but often has a higher fat content. It is used in mediterranean dishes, but can replace minced beef or turkey in other recipes if desired.

Pork Mince

Whilst not seen as traditional, pork mince can be a delicious alternative, particularly with tomato based sauces - simply remove the skin from sausages and voila, tasty pork mince.

So whichever minced meat you use, you're guaranteed to enjoy a delicious meal, and if it's the first time you've tried using mince, it certainly won't be your last!

Cottage Pie (Serves 4)

Ingredients

560g/1 1/4 lb lamb mince

1 tbsp oil

1 large onion, chopped

2 medium carrots, chopped

400g/14oz can tomatoes

290ml/10fl oz beef stock

1 bay leaf

fresh thyme leaves from 1 sprig

2 tbsps tomato purée

salt & freshly ground black pepper

Ingredients - for the topping

750g/1 1/2 lb potatoes, peeled and chopped

225g/8oz parsnips, peeled and chopped

2 tsps creamed horseradish

75g/2 1/2oz butter

55ml/2fl oz milk

Directions

1. Preheat the oven to 190°C/375°F/Gas mark 5. Heat the oil in a large pan. Add the onion and carrot and cook over a medium heat for 5 minutes until soft.

Cottage Pie/Cont.

2. Add the minced lamb and cook for 3 minutes to brown. Add the tomatoes, purée, beef stock, bay leaf and thyme. Cover and simmer for 30 minutes. Season.

3. Make the mash by boiling the potatoes and parsnips in water until soft. Drain and mash with the butter and milk. Stir in the horseradish and season with salt and pepper.

4. Spoon the meat into an ovenproof dish. Top with the mash and bake for 30 minutes until golden brown.

Cumberland Pie (Serves 6)

Ingredients

500g/17oz minced beef
1 beef stock cube, made up to 200ml/ with boiling water
1 tbsp oil
1 onion, chopped
1 tbsp plain flour
1.5 kg/3 1/2 lbs potato
15g/1 tbsp butter

Directions

1. Preheat the oven to 180°C/350°F/Gas mark 4.

2. Heat the oil in a shallow pan, and brown the onion, carrots and minced beef, stirring often.

3. Stir in the plain flour and then pour on the beef stock. Simmer for 10 minutes and adjust the seasoning, transfer to a suitable sized ovenproof dish.

4. Peel and dice the potato, and cook in boiling water until tender.

5. Mash the potato with the butter and use to top the minced beef in a pie dish. Fork the top attractively.

6. Bake for 40 minutes until golden, serve with a selection of freshly cooked vegetables.

Lamb Rissoles with Spicy Tomato Dip (Serves 2)

Ingredients

225g/8oz lean lamb mince
1 garlic clove, peeled and crushed
2 tbsps tomato ketchup
1 tbsp capers, finely chopped
25g/1oz breadcrumbs
salt & freshly milled black pepper
1 beaten egg

Ingredients - for the dip:

1 tsp oil
2 tbsps mayonnaise
2 tbsps tomato ketchup
1 tsp sweet chilli sauce

Directions

1. In a bowl mix together the lamb, garlic, tomato ketchup, capers and breadcrumbs. Mix well, season and shape into 6 rissoles.

2. Spread the breadcrumbs onto a plate, and dip each rissole into beaten egg and then into the breadcrumbs.

3. Cook for 8-10 minutes each side, under a preheated grill or by heating the oil in pan and frying. To make the dip, mix together the mayonnaise with the tomato ketchup and sweet chilli sauce.

4. Serve as a snack with toasted pitta bread, the tomato dip and salad or as a main meal with potato wedges.

Mama's Mince Bake (Serves 4)

Ingredients

225g/8oz minced beef
50g/2oz bacon, chopped
1 onion, chopped
1 carrot, chopped
1 stick celery, sliced
1 clove garlic, skinned and crushed
2 tbsps tomato puree
225ml/8fl oz stock
225g/8oz macaroni, cooked
225g/8oz peas
50g/2oz flour
50g/2oz butter
568ml/1 pint fresh milk
50g/2oz Double Gloucester cheese, grated
salt & freshly ground pepper

Directions

1. Dry fry the beef in a non-stick pan, add bacon, onion, carrots, celery, garlic, tomato, puree and stock. Bring to boil, cover and simmer gently for 1 hour.

2. Mix the meat, macaroni and peas. Place in an ovenproof dish.

3. Place flour, butter and milk in a saucepan, heat stirring until sauce thickens, boils and is smooth. Cook for a minute. Remove from heat, add half of cheese and stir until melted. Season.

4. Pour over the beef, sprinkle with remaining cheese and bake at 180°C/350°F/Gas mark 4 for 30 minutes.

Meat Loaf (Serves 4)

Ingredients

675g/1 1/2 lb minced beef
1 onion, finely chopped
1 tbsp chopped parsley
100g/4 oz fresh white breadcrumbs
1 egg, lightly beaten
2-3 tbsps red wine
salt & pepper
1 tbsp oil
1 onion, finely chopped
2 cloves garlic, crushed
400g/14 oz can chopped tomatoes
150ml/1/4 pint beef stock
1 tbsp chopped parsley
sliced pickled cucumber to garnish (optional)

Directions

1. Grease a 1 kg/2 lb loaf tin. Mix the mince, onion, parsley, breadcrumbs, egg, red wine and seasoning together thoroughly. Pack firmly into the tin and cover with a sheet of greased foil.

2. Bake in a moderate oven for 1 - 1 1/4 hours or until the loaf begins to shrink from the tin.

3. Heat the oil in a saucepan and cook the onion and garlic until soft.

4. Blend the tomatoes in a liquidiser and add to the onion mixture with the stock, parsley and seasoning to taste.

5. Bring the sauce to the boil, reduce the heat and simmer for 10 - 15 minutes, stirring occasionally, until the sauce has thickened.

6. Tip the meat loaf out of the tin and arrange on a serving dish, then pour over the hot tomato sauce.

Mince & Sweet Potato Mash (Serves 4)

Ingredients

675g/1 1/2 lbs lean minced beef
2 tbsps olive oil or sunflower oil
1 onion, finely chopped
1 carrot, finely diced
1-2 cloves garlic, crushed
400g/14oz tinned chopped tomatoes
3 tbsps tomato ketchup
2 tsps Worcestershire sauce
1/2 tsp dried thyme
black pepper

Ingredients - for the mash

1kg/2 1/4 lbs sweet potato
2 tbsps olive oil
1 tbsp fresh ginger, chopped
1 red chilli, deseeded & chopped
1 tbsp chopped coriander

Directions

1. Heat the oil in a pan over a medium heat and gently fry the onion and the carrot until softened and lightly coloured. Add the garlic and stir.

2. Increase the heat to high and add half the mince. Fry briskly, breaking up the lumps until it is lightly browned. Transfer the cooked meat to a plate.

3. Add the remaining mince to the pan and fry in the same way. When it is cooked, return the first batch to the pan and add the chopped tomatoes and all the remaining ingredients. Add 300ml of water. Bring up to the boil and half cover. Simmer the mixture gently, stirring from time to time, for about half an hour, adding more hot water as needed.

4. In the meantime, peel and cube the sweet potato, then boil in water until tender. Drain well then push through a vegetable mill or potato ricer. Heat 2 tbsps of olive oil in a small pan. Add the chopped ginger and red chilli. Fry for a couple of minutes until soft. Stir the ginger, chilli and oil into the mash along with the chopped coriander.

5. By this time the meat should be tender and most of the liquid should have evaporated away to leave a delicious moist mince stew.

Minced Beef Pie (Serves 4)

Ingredients

500g/1lb 2oz beef mince

2 tbsps vegetable oil

1 onion, chopped

1 tbsp tomato purée

1 1/2 tbsps plain flour, plus extra for dusting

75g/2 1/2oz mushrooms, chopped

250ml/9fl oz stout or beef stock

dash Worcestershire sauce

400g/14oz ready-made shortcrust pastry

1 free-range egg, yolk only, lightly beaten

Directions

1. Heat the oil in a deep frying pan and fry the beef mince for 4-5 minutes, breaking it up with a wooden spoon as it browns.

2. Add the onion and cook for 2-3 minutes, then stir in the tomato purée and cook for 2-3 more minutes. Stir in the flour and cook for a further minute, then add the chopped mushrooms, the stout or beef stock and a couple of dashes of Worcestershire sauce.

3. Bring to the boil, then reduce the heat, cover the pan with a lid and leave to simmer for 20 minutes. Set aside and leave to cool, then turn the meat mixture into a one litre pie dish.

4. Roll out the pastry on a floured work surface until it is slightly larger than the pie dish. Gently drape the pastry over the dish, pressing firmly onto the edges. Trim, then shape the edges into a fluted shape.Cut some leaf shapes out of the pastry trimmings and decorate the top of the pie, sticking them to the pastry with the beaten egg yolk.

5. Make three or four slits in the pastry to allow the steam to escape, then brush the pie with the rest of the beaten egg yolk and bake in the oven for 20-25 minutes, or until golden-brown.

Open Cornish pasties (Serves 4)
Ingredients

175g/6oz minced beef
sea salt & freshly ground black pepper
1 onion, chopped
4 tbsps tomato purée

Ingredients - for the pastry

140g/5oz self-raising flour, plus extra to dust
sea salt & freshly ground black pepper
2 tbsps olive oil
milk, to bind
butter, to grease
1 tsp fresh thyme leaves

Directions

1. Preheat the oven to 220°C/425°F/Gas mark 7. For the filling, heat a large pan over a medium to high heat and add the mince. Season with sea salt and freshly ground black pepper and cook for 3-4 minutes, stirring regularly, to brown the mince all over. Add the onion and tomato purée and fry for five minutes.

2. Meanwhile, for the pastry, place the flour in a bowl, season with sea salt and freshly ground black pepper. Add the olive oil and with clean hands mix together, adding milk gradually to form a dough.

3. Lightly dust a board with flour and roll out the pastry to a 20cm/8in by 30cm/12in size. Carefully place onto a swiss roll tin, greased with butter.

4. Spoon the mince mixture into the centre of the pastry, leaving a 5cm/2in border, then fold up the border over the edges of the mince.

5. Sprinkle over the thyme leaves and place in to the oven, and bake for 15 minutes, or until the pastry is golden. Serve immediately.

Puff Pastry Mince Roll (Serves 6)

Ingredients

368g/3oz packet frozen puff pastry

2 onions

1 small leek

100g/4oz mushrooms

450g/1 lb mixed minced meat

1 tbsp butter

2 egg yolks

salt & freshly milled white pepper

1 tsp soy sauce

100g/4 oz Gouda cheese

1 egg, separated

350g/12oz white cabbage

Directions

1. Defrost the pastry. Dice the onions. Trim, wash and cut the leek into rings and the cabbage into fine strips.

2. Trim, wash and finely slice the mushrooms. Fry the onion and minced meat in the butter in a large frying pan. Add the vegetables and braise for 10 minutes, stirring frequently.

3. Remove the minced meat and vegetables from the heat and work in the egg yolks, salt and pepper and the soy sauce. Finely dice the cheese.

4. Roll out the pastry into a large rectangle and spread it with the meat mixture, leaving 2.5 cm (1 in) pastry around the edges. Sprinkle with the cheese.

5. Brush the pastry edges with beaten egg white and roll up the pastry, pressing the edges lightly together.

6. Place the roll on a baking sheet and brush with egg yolk. Bake for 35 minutes in a moderately hot oven (200°C,/400°F/Gas mark 6) and serve hot.

Savoury Mince with Mushrooms (Serves 4)
Ingredients
500g/1.2lbs minced beef
2 tbsps vegetable oil
1 medium onion, chopped
1 green pepper, chopped
250g/9oz mushrooms, sliced
30g/1oz brown sugar
20ml tomato paste
1 tsp paprika
400g/14oz baked beans
100ml/4fl oz water
fresh chives, chopped

Directions

1. Heat oil in a frying pan and sauté the mince for 2 - 3 minutes. Add the onion and cook for another 2 minutes. Add the remaining ingredients, except the beans and chives. Add the water, cover and bring to the boil. Reduce the heat and let simmer for 20 minutes.

2. Add the beans, stir and heat through. Season to taste and sprinkle with the chives. Serve with boiled rice.

Savoury Pork Mince (Serves 4)
Ingredients
500g/1.2lb pork mince
1 large onion finely, chopped
1 tbsp curry powder
1 large garlic clove, crushed
1 tbsp oil
1/4 small cabbage, finely shredded
1 large carrot finely, chopped
100g/4oz green beans, chopped
1/2 red pepper, chopped
75g/3oz white rice
2 tbsps soy sauce
250ml/9fl oz chicken stock
salt & pepper to taste

Directions

1. Heat the oil over a medium heat and cook the onion, garlic and curry powder until the onion is slightly transparent.

2. Add the pork mince and break up with a fork, stirring until brown. Add the vegetables and rice, stirring to combine. Add the stock and soy sauce, stir in well, reduce heat and cook slowly until rice is tender.

3. Add the extra stock during cooking if required. Savoury mince should be moist, not dry and rice tender. Serve with rice or pasta.

Shepherd's Pie (Serves 4)
Ingredients

450g/1 lb minced beef
1 1/2 tbsps oil
1 onion, chopped
1 green pepper, deseeded & chopped
100g/4 oz mushrooms, sliced
2 tbsps tomato puree
1 tsp Worcestershire sauce
300ml/1/2 pint beef stock
salt & pepper
675g/1 1/2 lb potatoes
25g/1 oz butter or margarine
2-3 tbsps milk

Directions

1. Heat the oil in a frying pan and cook the onion and pepper for a few minutes. Stir in the minced beef and cook until it is evenly browned.

2. Add the mushrooms and cook until soft. Mix in the tomato puree, Worcestershire sauce, beef stock and seasoning and slowly bring the mixture to the boil. Reduce the heat and simmer gently for 20 minutes.

3. Meanwhile, cook the potatoes in a pan of boiling salted water for 20 minutes or until tender. Drain, mash with a fork, add the butter or margarine and the milk and beat until smooth.

Shepherd's Pie/Cont.

4. Place the meat mixture in an ovenproof dish and cover with the mashed potato, forking it neatly or piping it.

5. Bake in a moderate oven for 20 minutes or until the top is crisp and golden.

Spicy Meat Fritters (Makes 30)

Ingredients

450g/1 lb potatoes, boiled and drained
450g/1 lb lean minced beef
1 onion, quartered
1 bunch spring onions, chopped
3 garlic cloves, crushed
1 tsp ground nutmeg
1 tbsp coriander seeds, dry-fried and ground
2 tsps cumin seeds, dry-fried and ground
4 eggs, beaten
oil for shallow-frying
salt & freshly ground black pepper

Directions

1. While the potatoes are still warm, mash them in the pan until they are well broken up. Add to the minced beef and mix well together.

2. Finely chop the onion, spring onions and garlic. Add to the meat with the ground nutmeg, coriander and cumin. Stir in enough beaten egg to give a soft consistency which can be formed into fritters. Season to taste.

3. Heat the oil in a large frying pan. Using a dessertspoon, scoop out 6-8 oval-shaped fritters and drop then into the hot oil. Allow to set, so that they keep their shape (this will take about 3 minutes) and then turn over and cook for a further minute.

4. Drain well on kitchen paper and keep warm while cooking the remaining fritters

Steak Tartare (Serves 2)

Ingredients

200g/7oz fillet steak, minced
4 tbsps finely chopped red onion
4 tbsps finely chopped courgette
salt & freshly ground black pepper

Directions

1. Mix the mince together with the onion and courgette and season well with salt and freshly ground black pepper.

2. To serve, place an oiled chefs' ring into the middle of a plate, press the mince into the ring then remove. Serve.

Yorkshire Puddings with Minced Beef & Horseradish (Serves 4)

Ingredients

4oz/115g plain flour
pinch of salt
150ml/1/4 pint semi-skimmed milk
2 tbsps virgin olive oil
1 egg

Ingredients - for the filling

450g/1 lb lean minced beef
450ml/3/4 pint beef stock
2 large onions
1 tbsp olive oil
1 large carrot
4 tbsps horseradish relish
1 tbsp Worcestershire sauce
a few drops gravy browning (optional)
salt & freshly ground black pepper
parsley sprigs for garnish

Directions

1. Sift the flour and a pinch of salt into a bowl. Beat in the egg, milk and 1/4 pint (150 ml) of cold water, to give a smooth batter.

2. Place a teaspoon of oil in each of the Yorkshire pudding tins. Place in the oven for 2 - 3 minutes, until very hot. Divide the batter between the tins and bake for 40 minutes (30 minutes for smaller ones) until risen.

3. Meanwhile, chop the onions and saute them in 1 tablespoon of olive oil until transparent. Add the minced beef and cook until well browned on all sides. Stir in the stock and simmer for about 10 minutes. Grate the carrot ready for the garnish.

4. Stir in the horseradish relish, Worcestershire sauce, and a few drops of gravy browning if wished. The mixture should be moist with the stock, but not sloppy. Season to taste.

5. Fill the Yorkshire puddings with the minced beef and top each one with a little grated carrot. Garnish each pudding with a sprig of parsley and serve.

American Sloppy Joes (Serves 6)

Ingredients

1 small onion, diced finely
450g/1 lb beef mince
4 tbsps of tomato ketchup
1-2 tbsps mustard
1 tsp oil
salt & pepper to taste

Directions

1. In a large frying pan sautéfthe onion until tender. Add beef and cook until brown.

2. Drain the oil and reduce to a low heat. Add the ketchup, mustard, salt and pepper and stir. Heat through.

3. Serve on hamburger style buns.

Basic Burger (Serves 4)

Ingredients

500g/1.2lbs mince
1 tsp dried herbs
salt & ground black pepper
1 tbsp vegetable oil
4 burger buns

Directions

1. Mix the mince with the herbs and season. Divide into four, and shape into burgers. Heat the oil in a large frying pan and fry the burgers for about 5 minutes each side, until cooked through.

2. Serve in buns, with salad.

Blue Cheese Burgers (Serves 4)

Ingredients

750g/1 1/2 lb lean minced beef
1 small onion, finely grated
1 tbsp tomato ketchup
salt & freshly ground black pepper
75g/3 oz Danish Blue cheese, mashed
2 tbsps vegetable oil

Directions

1. In a large bowl, mix together the minced beef, onion and tomato ketchup and season well with salt and pepper. Cover the mixture and refrigerate for 1 hour.

2. Divide the mashed cheese into 4 portions. Shape each portion into a ball and flatten slightly. Divide the chilled beef mixture into 4 portions and mould a portion around each ball of cheese.

3. Shape into a fairly thick hamburger, making sure that the cheese is completely enclosed by the meat mixture.

4. Heat the oil in a large frying-pan, add the hamburgers and fry for about 5-8 minutes on each side, until they are done to your liking.

5. Remove the hamburgers from the pan with a fish slice, drain quickly on absorbent paper and serve at once.

Burger with Beetroot Salsa (Serves 4)

IngredientsFor the salsa

250g/9oz baby beetroot
1/2 medium red onion, finely chopped
1 tsp ground cumin
1 tbsp freshly chopped coriander
2 tbsps olive oil

IngredientsFor the burgers

450g/1 lb beef mince
salt & freshly milled black pepper
1 medium egg, lightly beaten

To serve

4 ciabatta rolls
50g rocket
4 tbsps mayonnaise

Directions

1. Preheat the grill to high. Chop the beetroot into small cubes. Place in a bowl with the onion, cumin, coriander and oil. Season, mix well and set aside.

2. Place the mince in a mixing bowl with the egg and some seasoning. Use your hands to form the mixture into 4 burger shapes. Chill until ready to cook.

3. When ready to cook, place the burgers on a foil-lined baking tray or grill pan and cook for 6-8 minutes on each side until thoroughly cooked, the juices run clear and there is no pink meat. Then split and lightly toast the rolls.

4. Place a handful of rocket leaves on the base of each roll and top with a burger, some mayonnaise and some beetroot salsa. Replace the tops and serve with the spicy potato wedges or chunky fries.

Chipotle Beefburgers (Serves 6)

Ingredients

2 tbsps sunflower oil
1 onions, finely chopped
2 cloves garlic, crushed
3 tsps Chipotle Paste
1/2 tsp ground cumin
500g/17oz beef mince
1 medium egg, lightly beaten
2 tsps fresh flat leaf parsley, finely chopped

Directions

1. Heat half the oil in a small frying pan and sauté the onions for 4–5 minutes until softened. Add the garlic and cook for 1 minute. Add the chipotle paste and cumin, and gently fry for 1–2 minutes. Remove from the heat and leave to cool.

2. Place the beef in a mixing bowl with the egg, parsley and some seasoning. Stir in the cooled onion mixture and mix again. Use your hands to form the mixture into 6 burger shapes. Chill until ready to cook.

3. Heat the remaining oil in a frying or griddle pan and cook the burgers for 8–10 minutes, turning once, until they are thoroughly cooked through with no pink meat. Alternatively, cook on a preheated barbecue.

4. Serve the burgers in lightly toasted sesame-seed burger buns, together with torn Romaine lettuce leaves and tomato slices, with a dollop of tomato ketchup on the side.

Chorizo Burgers (Serves 4)
Ingredients

220g/8oz chorizo sausages
250g/9oz minced pork
olive oil, for brushing
2 red peppers
4 pitta breads
rocket leaves

Ingredients - For the aioli

1 garlic clove, crushed
1 tbsp lemon juice
1 tbsp extra virgin olive oil
3 tbsps mayonnaise

Directions

1. Make the aioli by beating the garlic, lemon juice and olive oil into the mayonnaise, then set aside until the burgers are ready.

2. Skin the chorizo and finely chop the meat, then combine with the pork mince, mixing well with your hands. Form into 4 burgers. Brush them with olive oil and cook for 5 minutes on each side until cooked.

3. Cut each red pepper vertically into 4 panels, then discard the seeds and core. Brush with olive oil and grill on both sides until well-marked.

4. Brush the pitta breads with olive oil and grill on one side until marked. Top each pitta with two pieces of roasted red pepper, a chorizo burger, and some rocket leaves. Serve with the aioli.

Kofta Burgers (Serves 4)

Ingredients

500g/19oz beef mince
2 tbsps curry paste
1 small onion, finely chopped
2 garlic cloves, finely chopped
large bunch fresh mint, finely chopped
salt and freshly ground black pepper

Directions

1. Combine all the ingredients in a large bowl and mix until well blended. Divide the mixture into 4 and, with wet hands to prevent sticking, shape into burgers. Brush the burgers with a little oil and chill for 20 minutes.

2. Preheat the grill or barbecue and cook the burgers for 6-8 minutes on each side until they are thoroughly cooked, the juices run clear and there is no pink meat. Serve with warm bread.

Mini Burgers in Pitta Pockets (Serves 8)

Ingredients

500g/19oz beef mince
1 red pepper, deseeded and finely chopped
1 yellow pepper, deseeded and finely chopped
shredded Romaine lettuce leaves
4 spring onions, finely chopped
2 tsps Worcestershire sauce
8 small pitta breads
cherry tomatoes
tomato ketchup

Directions

1. Light the barbecue or preheat the grill to high. Place the ground beef in a bowl and stir in the chopped peppers, salad onions and Worcestershire sauce. Season and mix well to combine. Divide the mixture into 8 and shape into small burgers.

2. Cook the burgers on the barbecue for 10-15 minutes, turning once, or under the grill for 5-7 minutes on each side until the burgers are cooked through and there is no pink meat.

3. Warm the pittas on the barbecue or under the grill, then make a slit along one side and open up to form a pocket. Stuff with lettuce and chopped cherry tomatoes, then add a burger. Serve straight away, with tomato ketchup.

Minty Lamb Burgers with Gooey Cheese (Serves 4)

Ingredients

450g/1 lb lean lamb mince
2 tbsps freshly chopped mint or mint jelly
salt & freshly milled black pepper
25g/1oz Brie

Ingredients - for the minty yoghurt

3 tbsps low-fat natural yoghurt
1 tbsp freshly chopped mint

Directions

1. In a bowl mix together the lamb with the mint. Divide into 4 and shape into burgers.

2. Cook on preheated grill or barbecue for 4-6 minutes on each side until cooked through. During the last 1-2 minutes of cooking time top each burger with 25g/1oz Brie cheese and allow to melt.

3. For the minty yoghurt mix together the yoghurt and the remaining fresh mint.

4. Serve the burgers on toasted ciabatta with roasted or barbecued peppers, drizzled with the minty yoghurt.

Nice n Spicy Burgers (Serves 4)

Ingredients

450g/16oz lean beef mince
2 garlic cloves, crushed
1 tsp tomato ketchup
1 tsp Dijon mustard
1 egg, lightly beaten
1 red chilli, finely chopped
1 small onion, finely diced
2 spring onions, sliced
handful basil leaves, chopped
chilli infused olive oil for trying

Ingredients To serve

4 burger rolls
sweet chilli sauce for serving, optional

Directions

1. In a large bowl mix together the mince, garlic, tomato ketchup, mustard, egg, chilli and onion until well blended.

2. Add the spring onions and basil to the mix and shape into four burger patties with your hands.

4. Heat a little of the chilli infused olive oil in a large non-stick frying pan and fry the burgers. Turn them once only, cooking for about 5-6 minutes each side. Serve in warm burger buns with chilli sauce for dipping.

Pork Burgers with Olive Sauce (Serves 4)

Ingredients

1kg sweet potatoes, peeled and cut into chunks
500g/19oz pork mince
2 small organic onions, finely chopped
2 rashers back bacon, finely chopped
1 apple, peeled, cored and grated
4 tbsps organic olive oil
200ml/7fl oz tub crème fraîche
75g/3oz black olives, pitted and finely chopped

Directions

1. Cook the sweet potatoes in boiling water for 15 minutes or until tender. Meanwhile, place the mince in a bowl with half the chopped onions and all the bacon and grated apple.

2. Season and mix together until the ingredients are evenly combined. Shape into 8 small balls and flatten into burger shaped patties.

3. Drain the sweet potatoes, return to the pan and mash until smooth. Beat in half of the olive oil and plenty of black pepper. Keep warm.

4. Heat the remaining oil in a frying pan and gently fry the patties for 5-6 minutes on each side until golden and cooked through. Drain, then transfer to a plate and keep warm.

5. Fry the remaining chopped onion in the pan for 2-3 minutes until softened, adding a little more oil if necessary.

6. Stir in 100ml cold water, scraping up the pan juices. Then add the crème fraîche and chopped olives and season to taste. Heat through gently and serve with the patties and sweet potato mash.

27

Spicy Lamb Burger (Serves 4-6)
Ingredients
800g/1 3/4 lbs minced lamb

1 small onion, finely chopped

2 cloves garlic, crushed

1 tsp cumin seeds, crushed

2 green chillies, finely chopped

1 tbsp fresh mint, chopped

1 tsp coriander seeds, crushed

1/2 tsp black pepper

1 tsp salt

Directions

1. Place the lamb in a large bowl and add the remaining ingredients. Mix it all together until just combined. This is best done by hand but don't over-work the mixture or you'll get a tough burger. Wet you hands then shape the mixture into four burgers about 200g each or six smaller burgers.

2. The burgers can now be cooked either on a griddle pan or non-stick frying pan with a bit of oil, during the summer time it is fun to cook these on the barbeque. Make sure you pre-heat the fying pan, griddle pan or barbeque to a medium heat.

3. Cook the burgers for about 5 minutes on each side, turning them once only. Serve with burger buns and salad.

Spicy Turkey Burger (Serves 4)
Ingredients
500g/1lb 2oz turkey mince

3 tbsps Thai sweet chilli sauce

zest and juice 1 lime

1 red chilli, deseeded and finely chopped

100g/4oz sweetcorn

1/2 tsp ground coriander

2 tsps Thai fish sauce

large pinch ground cumin

40g/1 1/2oz breadcrumbs

large handful coriander leaves, chopped

Directions

1. Combine all of the ingredients in a bowl, season and mix with your hands. Divide into 4 and form each into a thick patty. Chill uncovered in the fridge for 1 hour, or cover with clingfilm and leave in the fridge overnight.

2. Oil the burgers. Grill on a hot griddle pan or barbecue for 15 minutes, turning once, until piping hot all the way through.

Stilton & Bacon Burger (Serves 8)
Ingredients

1 kg/2 1/4 lbs minced beef
1 small onion, finely chopped
4 tbsps fine bread crumbs
1 egg, lightly beaten
1 chilli, finely chopped
1 tsp salt
1 tsp mustard power or mustard
1/2 tsp black pepper
2 cloves garlic, crushed
8 burger buns

For the topping

200g/7oz Stilton
8 rashers of back bacon

Directions

1. Place the beef in a large bowl and add the remaining ingredients. Mix it all together until just combined. This is best done by hand but don't over-work the mixture or you'll get a tough burger.

2. Wet you hands then shape the mixture into burgers by flattening the mixture in your hand about 2cm or 1 inch thick and smoothing the edges.

3. The burgers can now be cooked either on a griddle pan, non-stick frying pan with a bit of oil, or even a barbeque. Make sure you pre-heat the frying pan, griddle pan or barbeque to a medium heat.

Stilton & Bacon Burger/Cont.

4. Cook the burgers for about 5 minutes on each side, turning them once only. In the meantime, grill the bacon until crispy. Place each burger on a bun, then put a rasher on top of each burger. Finally, crumble the Stilton evenly over the burgers and finish with the lid of the bun.

Tikka Turkey Burgers with Raita (Serves 4)
Ingredients

500g/19oz turkey breast mince
1 onion, finely chopped
4 tbsps Masala curry paste
2 tbsps natural yogurt
1 tbsp mango chutney
3 tbsps chopped fresh coriander
oil, for brushing
4 naan bread

For the raita

250ml/8fl oz natural yoghurt
1/2 cucumber, grated or finely chopped
large handful mint leaves, chopped
large pinch salt

Directions

1. In a large bowl, mix together the onion, tikka paste, yoghurt and mango chutney. Stir in the turkey mince, coriander and seasoning and mix until all ingredients are well combined.

2. Divide the mixture into 4 and, with wet hands to prevent sticking, shape into burgers. Brush the burgers with a little oil and chill for 20 minutes.

3. Preheat the grill or barbecue and cook the burgers for 6-8 minutes on each side until they are thoroughly cooked, the juices run clear and there is no pink meat.

4. Meanwhile, combine the ingredients for the raita in a bowl and mix well. When the burgers are cooked, serve in warm Naan Breads with a spoonful of raita on the side.

Hungarian-style Meatballs (Serves 4)

Ingredients

340g/12oz minced turkey
30g/1oz butter
1 small onion, finely chopped
340g/12oz mushrooms, finely chopped
50g/1 3/4oz fresh breadcrumbs
1 egg, beaten
2 tbsps chopped parsley
500g/1 lb small new potatoes
salt & pepper
4 tbsps plain low-fat yoghurt to serve
fresh flat-leaf parsley to garnish
paprika and pepper sauce
2 tbsps extra virgin olive oil
1 onion, finely chopped
2 garlic cloves, crushed
1 red pepper, seeded and thinly sliced
1 green pepper, seeded and thinly sliced
1 tbsp paprika
1 litre/1 3/4 pints of passata
pinch of caraway seeds

Directions

1. Melt the butter in a heavy-based frying pan. Add the onion and mushrooms, and cook over a moderate heat, stirring frequently, for about 10 minutes. Transfer the mixture to a bowl and allow it to cool slightly.

2. Add the minced turkey to the mushroom mixture and use a fork to break up the mince. Add the breadcrumbs, egg, parsley and a little salt and pepper.

Hungarian-style Meatballs/Cont.

3. Mix the ingredients until thoroughly combined. Wet your hands to prevent the mixture from sticking to them, then shape it into 20 walnut-sized balls. Set aside.

4. To prepare the sauce, heat the oil in a large flameproof casserole. Add the onion and cook for 4–5 minutes, stirring frequently, until softened but not browned.

5. Add the garlic and red and green peppers, then continue to cook, stirring constantly, for 2–3 minutes. Stir in the paprika and cook for 1 minute, then pour in the passata and bring to the boil over a high heat.

6. Stir in the caraway seeds and salt and pepper to taste. Add the meatballs and the potatoes to the simmering sauce, taking care not to break up the meatballs.

7. Bring the sauce back to simmering point, then cover and simmer gently for 35 minutes or until the potatoes are tender. Taste and adjust the seasoning, if necessary.

8. Ladle the meatballs, potatoes and sauce into bowls and swirl a little yoghurt into each portion. Garnish with parsley and serve.

Meatballs & Peanut Sauce (Serves 4)

Ingredients

450g/1 lb minced beef
1 onion, grated
salt & pepper
50g/2 oz fresh white breadcrumbs
1 egg, lightly beaten
1 tbsp chopped parsley
2 tbsps plain flour
2 tbsps oil
1 clove garlic, crushed
2 tbsps crunchy peanut butter
150ml/1/4 pint natural yogurt
1 tsp chilli powder
pinch of cayenne
1 tsp chopped parsley to garnish

Directions

1. Mix together the meat, onion, seasoning, breadcrumbs, egg and parsley. Form the mixture into 18 small balls the size of marbles and roll in the flour. Combine the oil and the crushed garlic and brush the mixture over the meatballs.

2. Thread the meatballs on to oiled skewers and grill for 2 - 3 minutes, turn the skewers and grill for a further 2 - 3 minutes.

3. Melt the peanut butter over a gentle heat, add the remaining ingredients and cook gently until hot, but do not let the sauce boil. Serve the meatballs on a bed of mixed salad.

4. Serve the sauce separately, garnished with chopped parsley.

Meatballs in Sweet and Sour Sauce (Serves 4)
Ingredients

450g/1 lb minced beef
1 small onion, chopped
1 tbsp chopped parsley
salt & pepper
1 egg, beaten
3 to 4 tbsps oil

For the sauce

2 tbsps vinegar
2 tbsps soy sauce
2 tbsps tomato ketchup
300ml/1/2 pint water
1 tbsp corn flour (corn starch)
2 tbsps light brown sugar

Directions

1. Mix together the beef, onion, parsley, salt and pepper and bind with the egg.

2. Divide into 12 or 16 portions and shape into small balls.

Meatballs in Sweet and Sour Sauce/Cont.

3. Heat the oil in a frying pan and add the meat balls. Cook gently, turning occasionally, until they are browned on all sides and cooked through.

4. Meanwhile, mix together all the sauce ingredients in a saucepan.

5. Bring to the boil, stirring, and simmer until clear and thickened.

6. Drain the meat balls and turn them into a warmed serving dish.

7. Pour over the sauce and serve with creamed potatoes, boiled rice or noodles.

Persian Meatballs with Cherry Rice (Serves 4)

Ingredients

500g/19 oz minced lamb
400g/16 oz Basmati rice
200g/8 oz dried cherries
1 onion, grated
3–4 tsps ground cinnamon
2–3 tbsps oil
1/4 tsp saffron
75g/3 oz butter, melted
3 tbsps almonds, roughly chopped
3 tbsps pistachios, roughly chopped

Directions

1. Wash the rice in a bowl of warm water, then rinse in a sieve under cold, running water. Cover the cherries with cold water and leave them to soak for 15 minutes.

2. Put the mince and grated onion in a bowl, season and add the cinnamon. Mix well and knead to a soft paste, then roll into little balls the size of cherries. Fry them in the sunflower oil over a medium heat for about 8 minutes, shaking the pan to brown all over.

3. Bring a large, heavy-bottomed pan of salted water to the boil and add the drained rice. Cook for 10 minutes, or until the rice is almost cooked but retains a little bite. Drain and set aside.

4. Mix the saffron with a tablespoon of hot water. Heat 2 tablespoons of butter in the pan you used for the rice; stir in the saffron and its liquid, then combine with a ladleful of rice.

5. Spread this mixture over the bottom of the pan, then continue to alternate layers of rice, meatballs and drained cherries, finishing with a layer of rice on top. Pour over the remaining butter.

6. Cook, with the lid on, over a very low heat for 20–30 minutes until the rice is tender. Serve with warm flat bread or pitta.

Swedish Meatballs (Serves 4)

Ingredients

250g/10oz minced beef
250g/10oz minced pork
1 egg, lightly beaten
200-300ml/1 - 1 1/2 cups cream and water mix
2 1/2 tbsps finely-chopped onion
50g/2oz toasted breadcrumbs
2 boiled potatoes, chilled
4-5 tbsps butter, margarine or oil
8 tbsps of lingonberry jam
salt & pepper

Directions

1. Fry the onions, in a little butter over a medium heat until golden. Remove from the heat. In a large mixing bowl, mash the potatoes, breadcrumbs and onions together with a little water.

2. Add the egg, minced beef, pork and the cream and water mix a little at a time until the mixture is a moist consistency. Flavour generously with salt and pepper.

3. Using your hand, shape the mixture into the size of a golfball and place on a floured board. Flatten gently with a spatular until the meatballs are about 1 inch thick. Fry slowly in plenty of butter, until the juices run clear.

4. Serve the meatballs with freshly boiled potatoes and lingonberry jam. Lingonberry jam can be found in specialist food stores. You could use cranberry jam as an alternative.

Tangy Meatballs (Serves 6)

Ingredients

450g/1 lb mince beef
225g/1/2 lb mince pork
80g/1/2 cup finely chopped onion
3 tbsps finely chopped fresh corriander
70g/1/2 cup finely chopped bell pepper, red or green
55ml/1/4 cup ketchup
1 tsp Worcestershire sauce
1 egg, slightly beaten
1 tsp chili powder
1/2 tsp oregano
1/2 tsp garlic powder
1/2 tsp ground cumin
1/2 tsp salt
1/4 tsp pepper
75-100g/3/4 to 1 cup fine dry bread crumbs

For the sauce

2 tins chopped tomatoes
1 tsp chili powder
200g/4oz of passata tomato sauce

Directions

1. Line a shallow baking pan with foil. Heat oven to 200°C/400°F/Gas mark 6. Combine the meatball ingredients, adding enough bread crumbs to make a firm mixture.

2. Shape into 1 1/2-inch meatballs and arrange in one layer in the prepared pan. Bake for about 15 minutes. Remove and turn the meatballs, return to the oven and bake for 15 minutes longer.

3. Meanwhile, combine the sauce ingredients in a large saucepan. With a slotted spoon or tongs, add the meatballs to the sauce.

4. Cover and simmer for 15 to 20 minutes. Serve with hot cooked rice, with freshly baked cornbread and cooked beans on the side, if desired.

Traditional Italian Meatballs & Tagliatelle (Serves 4)

Ingredients

500g/1lb 2oz lean minced beef
2 tbsps extra virgin olive oil
3 tbsps water
2 garlic cloves, very finely chopped
handful of fresh flatleaf parsley, very finely chopped
salt & black pepper

To serve

400g/14 oz tagliatelle
20 cherry tomatoes, de-seeded and sliced
handful of flatleaf parsley

Directions

1. To make the meatballs, mix together the beef, garlic, parsley, half the olive oil and some salt and pepper. When all the ingredients are well combined, shape into about 40 small balls using wet hands to stop the mixture sticking to you!

2. To steam, half fill a pan with water and put it on the hob to boil. Cover with a plate roughly the same size as the pan, or just a little larger, and put the remaining half of the olive oil and the water on the plate.

3. When the water begins to boil, turn down the heat to medium, so the water is gently simmering. Place the meatballs on the plate on top of the pan and cover with an upturned plate, or ideally, a glass bowl so that you can see through it.

4. Leave it to steam for 30 minutes, turning the meatballs over halfway through. When the meatballs are cooked through, remove from the plate and pour the liquid into a pan.

5. Add the cooked pasta, cherry tomatoes and flatleaf parsley and toss until combined. Serve with the steamed meatballs.

Thai Meatballs with Noodles (Serves 4)

Ingredients

50g/2oz caster sugar
2 tbsps Thai fish sauce
1 stalk fresh lemon grass, finely chopped
1 small red chilli, deseeded and finely chopped
500g/19oz turkey breast mince
3 spring onions, finely chopped
1 tbsp cornflour
4 tbsps chopped fresh coriander
250g/10oz pack Egg Noodles
Thai sweet chilli dipping sauce
black pepper

Directions

1. Place the sugar and fish sauce in a small saucepan and heat gently until the sugar has dissolved. Remove from the heat and stir in the lemon grass and chilli. Allow to cool slightly.

2. Stir this mixture into the turkey mince with the salad onions (reserving a few for garnishing), cornflour, coriander and seasoning.

3. Using lightly-floured hands, shape the mixture into approximately 20 balls. Cover and chill in the fridge for at least 30 minutes.

4. Heat a little vegetable oil in a non-stick frying pan and gently fry the meatballs, turning occasionally, for approximately 15 minutes until thoroughly cooked, the juices run clear and there is no pink meat. Drain on a piece of kitchen paper.

5. Cook the noodles according to the pack instructions and serve with the meatballs, garnished with the reserved salad onions, and a bowl of chilli dipping sauce.

Turkey Meatballs (Serves 4)
Ingredients

500g/19oz minced turkey

1/2 onion, roughly chopped

1 clove garlic

1 red chilli, deseeded and roughly chopped

3cm-piece ginger, peeled and roughly chopped

grated zest of 1 lime

1 tsp sunflower oil

375g/15oz mixed vegetables for stir-frying

300ml/7fl oz chicken stock

3 tbsps soy sauce

2 tsps cornflour, blended to a paste with 1 tbsp water

1 tsp sesame oil

Directions

1. Put the first five ingredients in a food processor and mince finely. Transfer to a bowl and mix in the turkey. Season with salt and pepper. With wet hands, roll into walnut-sized balls.

2. Heat the oil in a wok over a medium-low heat and gently fry the meatballs until cooked (about 15 minutes). Set aside. Increase the heat under the pan, add the vegetables and fry until almost cooked.

3. Add the meatballs, stock and soy sauce. Add the cornflour, stir until thickened. Serve with rice or noodles, drizzled with the sesame oil.

Ultimate Tasty Meatballs (Serves 4)
Ingredients

400g/18oz lamb mince

2 tbsps fresh breadcrumbs

1 small onion, chopped finely

1 clove of garlic, chopped finely

1 tsp red chilli flakes

1 tsp dried oregano

1 tsp dried basil

2 tbsps Parmesan cheese, grated

1 egg, beaten
salt & pepper
olive oil as needed

For the sauce

300ml/1 1/4 cups tomato juice
400g/14oz tin chopped tomatoes
1 beef stock cube
small handful fresh basil
salt and pepper

1. In a large bowl, mix together the mince, onion, garlic, herbs, Parmesan, salt and pepper and the egg. When well combined, gradually squidge in the breadcrumbs until you have a firm, yet moist mixture that can be easily rolled into balls.

2. Dip your hands into a bowl of cold water and start rolling the mix into balls – re-dip your hands if the mixture starts to stick. If the balls are about an inch in diameter, you should be able to make about 20 meatballs. Place the meatballs on a platter and chill until needed.

3. Heat a couple of tablespoons of olive oil in a large frying pan over a medium heat. If your mince was quite fatty then you can probably get away with dry frying the meatballs. Fry the meatballs until browned on all sides. This is easiest if the pan is uncrowded and the meatballs are well chilled. If they're not chilled then they will break up very easily and while it still tastes good, it spoils the overall look of the dish.

4. Once all the meatballs are browned, pour over the tomato juice and chopped tomatoes. Crumble the stock cube over and add salt and pepper. Give it a gentle stir and leave to simmer uncovered for 30-35 minutes. By this time, the sauce should be thick and sweet. Adjust the seasoning if necessary and serve over fresh pasta.

Ultimate Meatball Baguette (Serves 4)

Ingredients

400g/18oz lamb mince
2 tbsps fresh breadcrumbs
1 small onion, chopped finely

Ultimate Meatball Baguette/Cont.

1 clove of garlic, chopped finely

1tsp red chilli flakes

1 tsp dried oregano

1 tsp dried basil

2 tbsps Parmesan cheese, grated

1 egg, beaten

salt & pepper

olive oil as needed

4 individual baguettes (or 2 large baguettes, halved).

For the sauce

300ml/1 1/4 cups tomato juice

400g/16oz tin chopped tomatoes

1 beef stock cube

small handful fresh basil

salt and pepper

For the filling

1 red onion, sliced

1 red pepper, deseeded & sliced

1 yellow pepper, deseeded & sliced

100g/4oz Mozzarella cheese

Directions

1. Follow the same method as the previous page to make the meatballs and sauce. In the meantime, in a little olive oil fry the red onion, red pepper and yellow pepper until softened. Remove from the heat and allow to cool slightly.

2. Warm the bread in the oven on a medium heat for about 5 minutes. Carefully split open the bread and ladle the meatballs on the bread, then add the onion and pepper mix. Lastly, top with mozzarella and flash under the grill until the cheese bubbles and browns.

Cannelloni au Gratin (Serves 4)

Ingredients

12 cannelloni
1 tbsp oil
100g/4oz streaky bacon, rinded and finely chopped
450g/1 lb minced steak
100g/4oz onions, skinned and finely sliced
60g/2 1/4 oz can tomato puree
1/2 tsp dried mixed herbs
40g/1 1/2oz butter
25g/1oz plain flour
450ml/3/4 pint milk
100g/4oz mature cheddar cheese, grated
salt & freshly ground pepper
pinch of freshly grated nutmeg
pinch of cayenne

Directions

1. Cook the cannelloni as directed on the packet, cool under running water and drain carefully.

2. Heat the oil in a frying-pan and fry the bacon until crisp. Add the minced steak and onion and fry until the meat is fully cooked.

3. Drain off any surplus fat then stir in the tomato puree and the herbs.

4. Using a teaspoon and standing the cooked cannelloni up on end, carefully fill. Grease an ovenproof dish and lay the cannelloni flat in the dish.

Cannelloni au Gratin/Cont.

5. Melt the butter in a saucepan and stir in the flour. Cook for 1 - 2 minutes. Remove from the heat and gradually stir in the milk. Return to the heat and bring to the boil. Cook for 2-3 minutes until thickened. Stir in the cheese and season with salt and pepper.

6. Pour the sauce over the cannelloni. Lightly sprinkle with the spices and bake in the oven at 200°C/400°F/Gas mark 6 for about 30 minutes until bubbling and golden.

Chilli Beef Pizza (Serves 4)
Ingredients
175g/7oz lean minced beef
1 large pizza base
1 small onion, thinly sliced
1 garlic clove, crushed
1/2 yellow pepper, chopped
1 tbsp olive oil
1/4 tsp hot chilli powder
1/4 tsp ground cumin
200g/1 cup tinned red kidney beans, drained
1 jar tomato sauce for pizza
2 tbsps Jalapeño chillies, sliced
3 tbsps Mozzarella cheese, thinly sliced
4 tbsps mature Cheddar cheese, grated
olive oil for drizzling
salt and black pepper, to taste
chopped parsley, to garnish

Directions

1. Gently fry the onion, garlic and yellow bell pepper in the olive oil for about 5 minutes until soft but not browned. Increase the heat very slightly then add the beef, chilli powder and cumin. Fry for 5 minutes more, stirring occasionally. Remove from the heat and stir-in the kidney beans before seasoning and setting aside.

2. Spread the tomato sauce over the top of the pizza then top with the meat mixture. Top with the sliced chillies and Mozzarella before scattering the grated Cheddar over everything. Drizzle a little olive oil over the top then season well.

3. Place in an oven pre-heated to 180°C/350°F/Gas mark 4 and bake for about 18 minutes, or until the crust is risen and golden.

4. Remove from the oven and sprinkle the chopped parsley over the top and serve immediately.

Fiery Pepper Dip with Crispy Lamb (Serves 2)

Ingredients

250g/10oz lamb mince
1 onion, finely chopped
1/2 tsp ground cinnamon
1/2 tsp cumin seeds

Ingredients - for the Moroccan dip

400g can/16oz chickpeas, drained and rinsed
juice of 1 lemon
4 canned piquillo peppers
2 tbsps tahini
1 clove garlic, thinly chopped
120ml/1/2 cup olive oil
black pepper

To serve

olive oil, for drizzling
pitta bread, griddled
chopped fresh parsley

Fiery Pepper Dip with Crispy Lamb/Cont.
Directions

1. In a food processor combine the chickpeas, lemon juice, peppers, tahini paste, and garlic. Pulse until smooth. With the machine running, slowly add 100ml of the olive oil. Season with salt and freshly ground black pepper.

2. Heat the remaining olive oil in a frying pan over a moderate heat and fry the onions slowly until they begin to caramelise. Sprinkle with the ground cinnamon and cumin seeds and then add the lamb mince. Cook the mixture until the mince is crispy and well browned, and then season with salt and freshly ground black pepper.

3. Spoon the dip into the centre of a large platter and drizzle with olive oil. Spoon the crispy lamb over the dip and arrange freshly griddled pita bread around the dish. Garnish with parsley and serve immediately.

Gnocchi Bolognese Bake (Serves 6)

Ingredients

500g/1 lb 2oz minced beef
1 onion, chopped
1-2 cloves garlic, finely chopped
250g/10oz mushrooms, cleaned and sliced
500g/1 lb 2oz gnocchi
350g/14oz Quattro Formaggi Cheese Sauce
3 tbsps grated mozzarella
450g/1 lb pasta sauce or passatta

Directions

1. Preheat the oven to 180°C/350°F/Gas mark 4. Place the minced beef, onion and garlic in a nonstick pan and fry gently for 5-6 minutes, stirring all the time, until the onion is starting to soften.

2. Stir in the mushrooms and cook for a further 5-6 minutes until the meat is browned. Pour over the tomato and herb sauce, bring to the boil, season with black pepper, then cover and simmer for 15 minutes.

3. Meanwhile, cook the gnocchi in a pan of boiling water according to pack instructions. Drain well.

4. To assemble the dish, spoon half the Bolognese mixture into a large shallow ovenproof dish, then top with the gnocchi. Add the remaining Bolognese sauce and then spoon the cheese sauce over the top. Sprinkle with the mozzarella.

5. Bake on the top shelf of the oven for 30-35 minutes, until golden and bubbling.

Italian Meatball Casserole (Serves 4)

Ingredients

450g/1 lb lean minced beef
1 medium onion
salt & freshly ground black pepper
1 tbsp Worcestershire sauce

Ingredients - for the sauce

350g/12 oz large courgettes
1 large red pepper
115g/4 oz large button mushrooms
2 tbsps virgin olive oil
400g/14 oz can tomatoes
1 tsp dried oregano
2 tsps arrowroot powder

Directions

1. Peel and finely chop the onion, then combine all the ingredients for the meatballs in a large mixing bowl, adding 1 teaspoon of salt and 1/2 teaspoon of freshly ground black pepper. Shape the meat mixture into 24 balls, pressing each one firmly to hold its shape, then put them to one side.

2. Slice the courgettes. Halve and de-seed the red pepper and cut it into 1in (25mm) squares. Clean and slice the button mushrooms.

3. Heat the olive oil in a large frying pan or in a flameproof casserole with a tightly fitting lid, and brown the meatballs evenly over a medium heat for about 5 minutes.

4. Remove the meatballs from the pan and add the mushrooms to it, frying them quickly for 2 minutes. Return the meatballs to the pan and add the other vegetables, tomatoes and oregano. Gently bring to the boil, cover and simmer for 15 minutes.

5. Mix the arrowroot with 1 tablespoon of cold water until smooth, then stir it into the casserole and continue cooking over a moderate heat until the sauce has thickened. Serve immediately.

Lasagne (Serves 6)

Ingredients - for the white sauce

sea salt & freshly ground black pepper

700ml/3 cups skimmed milk

1 thick slice of onion

3 tbsps cornflour

freshly grated nutmeg

25g/1oz Parmesan cheese, grated

Ingredients - for the meat sauce

500g/1 lb minced beef

1 large onion, finely chopped

1 carrot, finely chopped

2 cloves garlic, crushed

400g/16oz can chopped tomatoes

2 tbsps tomato purée

3 tbsps red wine

1 tbsp fresh oregano, chopped (or 1 tsp dried)

1 bay leaf

sea salt & freshly ground black pepper

Directions

1. To make the meat sauce, put the beef, onion, carrot and garlic in a pan and cook over a medium heat, stirring, for about 5 minutes, until the meat is no longer pink. Spoon off any fat, but leave the juices.

2. Add the tomatoes, tomato purée, red wine, oregano, bay leaf and seasoning. Bring to the boil, reduce to a simmer, cover and cook gently for 30 minutes.

3. Meanwhile make the white sauce. Put all but 3 tbsps of the milk in a pan. Add the bay leaf and onion, bring to the boil, then remove from the heat and leave to stand for 15 minutes.

4. In a separate pan, mix the cornflour with the remaining milk. Strain the infused milk into the pan and bring to the boil. Simmer for 2 minutes, stirring continuously, until thickened. Season and add nutmeg to taste. Remove from the heat.

Lasagne/Cont.

5. Preheat the oven to 190°C/375°F/Gas mark 5. Cover the bottom of a medium-sized ovenproof serving dish with a single layer of lasagne sheets. Spoon on a thin layer of meat sauce, and cover with some of the white sauce.

6. Arrange a layer of lasagne on top of this. Continue layering, finishing with white sauce. Sprinkle with the grated Parmesan. Bake for 20-25 minutes, or until bubbling and golden on top. Serve immediately with a salad or green vegetables.

Moroccan Mince (Serves 4)

Ingredients

500g/1 lb 2oz beef mince
2-3 tbsps olive oil
1 clove garlic, crushed
125g/5oz pine nuts
125g/5oz raisins
1/2 tsp ground coriander
1-1/2 tsps ground cumin
1 tsp ground cinnamon
1 tsp ground chilli powder
100ml/1/2 cup chicken stock
pinch of black pepper

Directions

1. Heat the oil in a heavy nonstick pan over medium-high heat then add the mince, garlic, pine nuts, cumin and cinnamon.

2. Cook for 2-3 minutes, stirring constantly, until the mince is sealed and pine nuts are slightly golden. Add the raisins, chili powder, stock, and pepper.

3. Continue to cook 5-6 minutes, stirring constantly. Serve with couscous.

Moussaka (Serves 4)

Ingredients

675g/1 lb 8oz minced Lamb
4 tbsps olive oil
3 cloves garlic, finely chopped
1 onion, diced
2 aubergines, cut into chunks
3 plum tomatoes
284ml/1 1/4 cup chicken stock
pinch ground cinnamon
freshly grated nutmeg
1 tsp mint, chopped

Ingredients - for the sauce

50g/2oz butter
2 tbsps flour
440ml/2 cups milk
150g/5oz Gruyère cheese, grated
3 tbsps Parmesan, grated
2 eggs

Directions

1. Preheat the oven to 220°C/425°F/Gas mark 6. Heat 2 tablespoons of olive oil in a large frying pan. Add the garlic, aubergine and onion with the remaining olive oil and cook gently for 5 minutes.

2. Add the lamb and brown for 2-3 minutes, then add the tomatoes. Pour in the chicken stock and add the spices. Stir, bring to the boil and simmer for 10 minutes. Season the mixture with salt, pepper and add the mint. Spoon the mixture into a large baking dish.

3. To make the sauce, melt the butter in a pan. Stir in the flour, mixing well over a low heat and cook for 30-60 seconds. Gradually whisk in the milk, mixing thoroughly to ensure there are no lumps and continue cooking until smooth. Add the grated cheese and season with salt and pepper.

4. Remove from the heat and cool slightly. Whisk in the egg yolks. Pour the sauce over the lamb mixture and cook in the oven for 10 minutes until bubbling.

Pasta Bake (Serves 4)

Ingredients

450g/1 lb minced beef
1 red pepper, seeded and sliced
1 onion, skinned and chopped
100g/4oz button mushrooms, wiped and sliced
400g/14oz tin tomatoes, with juice
1 tsp Tabasco sauce
salt & freshly ground pepper
100g/4oz wholewheat spaghetti rings
300g/10oz natural yoghurt
1 egg, beaten
50g/2oz flour, sifted
2 tomatoes, sliced
chopped fresh parsley to garnish

Directions

1. In a saucepan, gently fry the mince in its own fat, until turning brown.

2. Drain off any fat. Add the pepper, onion, mushrooms, the tin of tomatoes and juice, Tabasco sauce and seasoning, Simmer gently for 10 minutes.

3. Meanwhile, cook the pasta in a pan of fast boiling water for about 10 minutes, until tender, but not soft. Drain.

4. Place in a 1.4 litres (2 1/2 pints) ovenproof dish. Top with the mince mixture.

5. Beat together the yoghurt, egg and flour until smooth, pour over the mince. Bake in the oven at 180°C/350°F/Gas mark 4 for 40 minutes. Serve hot, garnished with tomatoes and chopped parsley.

Pork Penne & Fennel Ragu (Serves 4)

Ingredients

400g/16oz pork mince
400g/16oz penne
1 tbsp fennel seeds

3 garlic cloves, sliced
1 lemon, finely grated zest
125ml/1/2 cup white wine
100ml/1/2 cup full-cream milk
3 tbsps double cream
1/4 tsp nutmeg, freshly grated
10 basil leaves
50g/2oz Parmesan, grated

Directions

1. Heat the olive oil in a frying pan and add the fennel seeds and the mince. Turn up the heat and use the back of your spoon to spread the pork mince out so it cooks and browns evenly. Cook for 3-4 minutes over a high heat until no traces of pink remain.

2. Bring a large pan of salted water to the boil and cook the pasta according to the packet instructions. Add the garlic and lemon zest to the mince in the pan and stir for one minute until the garlic softens. Slosh the white wine and milk into the mince mix and boil for 5 minutes until the liquid has almost disappeared.

3. Stir in the double cream and allow to simmer for 1-2 minutes. Taste, season as required and stir in the nutmeg and basil.

4. Drain the pasta, spoon the ragu into the bowl, toss with the pasta and basil and sprinkle the Parmesan on top.

Rose Beef Koftas (Serves 6)
Ingredients

500g/1 lb 2oz lean mince beef
1 tbsp olive oil
2 shallots, finely diced
1 tsp cumin seeds
1/2 tsp ground cinnamon
1 1/2 tsp Belazu Rose Harissa
1 tsps of Star Kay Rose Water,
1/2 tsp sea salt

Rose Beef Koftas/Cont.
Directions

1. Prepare and light the barbecue, or preheat the grill to high. Soak 6 long wooden skewers in cold water for at least 30 minutes. Warm the oil in a frying pan over a high heat. Add the shallots and fry for 5 minutes or until golden. Remove from the heat and add the cumin and cinnamon. Stir well to combine then set aside to cool completely.

2. Place the mince in a large bowl. Add the cooled onion mixture, harissa, rose water and a pinch of salt. Using your hands, knead the mixture for about 3 minutes or until well combined and smooth.

3. Divide the mixture into 6 even pieces. With dampened hands, shape each portion of mince around the prepared skewers until the mixture forms a 'sausage' about 17cm long.

4. Barbecue or grill the koftas for 8-10 minutes, turning them with tongs 2-3 times during cooking. Serve immediately with salad and dollops of Greek yogurt dusted with ground cinnamon.

Spaghetti Bolognese (Serves 4)
Ingredients

350g/12oz lean minced beef
1 tbsp olive oil
1 onion, finely chopped
2 garlic cloves, chopped
1 carrot, scraped and chopped
1 stick celery, chopped
50g/1 3/4oz pancetta or streaky bacon, diced
400g/14 oz can chopped tomatoes
2 tsps dried oregano
125ml/4 fl oz red wine

Directions

1. Heat the oil in a large frying pan (skillet). Add the onions and cook for 3 minutes.

2. Add the garlic, carrot, celery and pancetta or bacon and saute for 3-4 minutes or until just beginning to brown.

3. Add the beef and cook over a high heat for another 3 minutes or until all of the meat is brown.

4. Stir in the tomatoes, oregano and red wine and bring to the boil. Reduce the heat and leave to simmer for about 45 minutes.

5. Stir in the tomato puree (paste) and season with salt and pepper.

6. Cook the spaghetti in a pan of boiling water for 8 - 10 minutes until tender, but still has 'bite'. Drain thoroughly.

7. Transfer the spaghetti to a serving plate and pour over the bolognese sauce. Toss to mix well and serve hot.

Spiced Lamb Pittas with Quick Piccalilli (Serves 4)
Ingredients

450g/1 lb lean lamb mince

2 tbsps curry paste

1 garlic clove, peeled and crushed

Ingredients - for the quick piccalilli

2 gherkins, sliced

2.5cm/1 inch piece cucumber, sliced

3 cauliflower florets, broken into very small florets

1/4 red pepper, deseeded and thinly sliced

1 tbsp vinegar (from gherkin jar)

2 tbsps honey

1 tsp English mustard

Directions

1. To make the piccalilli mix together the gherkins, cucumber, cauliflower florets and red pepper. Add the vinegar honey and mustard.

2. Mix well, cover and leave flavours to infuse. You can allow the piccalili to ferment overnight in the fridge. Mix the mince with the curry paste and garlic. Shape into 20 small patties and cook under a preheated grill for approximately 10 minutes until cooked through. Serve with toasted pitta.

Spiced Mince with Sweet Potato Wedges (Serves 4)
Ingredients - for the spiced mince

1 tbsp olive oil

100g/3 1/2oz minced beef

1 clove garlic, chopped

1 tbsp chopped chives

2 tbsps chopped coriander

1 tbsp soy sauce

Ingredients - for the sweet potato wedges

1/2 sweet potato, cut into wedges

2 tbsps olive oil

salt & freshly ground black pepper

1 tbsp soy sauce

1 tbsp tomato ketchup
1 tsp Dijon mustard

Ingredients - for the yoghurt dip
100g/3 1/2oz yoghurt
1/2 clove garlic, chopped
handful of mint, chopped
salt & freshly ground black pepper

Directions

1. Preheat the oven to 200°C/400°F/Gas mark 6. Place the sweet potato wedges on a baking tray and drizzle with the oil. Season with salt and freshly ground black pepper, then place into the oven for 15 minutes. Remove from the oven and brush with the soy, ketchup and mustard.

2. In a hot non-stick pan, heat the oil, then add the beef and cook for 5 minutes until cooked through. Add the garlic and cook for a further 2 minutes. Finally add the chives, coriander and soy sauce. Take off the heat.

3. In a bowl mix the yoghurt with the garlic and mint, then season with salt and freshly ground black pepper. To serve, place the sweet potato wedges on the plate and top with the spiced beef and a dollop of the yoghurt dip.

Spicy Kebabs (Makes 18-20 balls)
Ingredients
450g/1 lb minced beef
1 egg
3 garlic cloves, crushed
1/2 onion, finely chopped
1/2 tsp freshly ground black pepper
1 1/2 tsp ground cumin
1 1/2 tsp ground coriander
1 tsp ground ginger
2 tsps garam masala
1 tbsp lemon juice
50-75g/2-3 oz fresh white breadcrumbs
1 small chilli, seeded and chopped
oil, for deep frying
salt

Spicy Kebabs/Cont.
Directions

1. Place the minced beef in a large bowl and add the egg, garlic, onion, spices, seasoning, lemon juice, about 50g (1 oz) of the breadcrumbs and the chilli.

2. Using your hands or a wooden spoon, mix the ingredients together until the mixture is firm. If it feels sticky, add more of the breadcrumbs and mix again until firm.

3. Heat the oil in a large heavy pan or deep-fat fryer. Shape the mixture into balls or fingers and fry, a few at a time, for 5 minutes or until well browned all over.

4. Using a slotted spoon, drain the kebabs and then transfer to a plate lined with kitchen paper. Cook the remaining kebabs in the same way and then serve.

Stuffed Aubergines (Serves 6)
Ingredients

315g/10 oz minced beef
6 small aubergines (egg plant)
1 onion, chopped
2 tsps cooking oil
1/2 tsp salt
freshly ground black pepper to taste
1 tsp Dijon mustard
125g/4 oz Cheddar cheese, grated

Directions

1. First prepare the aubergines by halving them lengthwise. To form hollows for the mince mixture, remove some of the flesh from the centre and reserve.

2. To prepare the mince, saute onion in heated cooking oil until translucent. Add mince and chopped reserved aubergine and fry until mince turns colour.

3. Add salt, pepper and remaining ingredients except Parmesan and parsley. Spoon some of the mixture into each hollowed-out aubergine.

4. Sprinkle Parmesan and parsley over and bake at 160°C/325°F/Gas mark 3 for 30 minutes.

Black Bean Chilli (Serves 4)

Ingredients

500g/1 lb 2oz minced beef
1 large onion, chopped
1 red pepper, deseeded & chopped
2 tsps dried oregano
1 tbsp chilli powder, to taste
2 x 400g cans chopped tomatoes
400g/16oz can Epicure Black Beans, drained and rinsed

Ingredients - To serve

8 soft corn tortillas
4 tbsps crème fraîche
25g/1 oz fresh coriander, roughly chopped

Directions

1. Place the onion and ground beef in a large pan and dry fry, stirring occasionally to break up the mince, until all the meat is browned. Add the red pepper and cook for a further 1-2 minutes.

2. Stir in the oregano and chilli powder, the chopped tomatoes and black beans. Bring to the boil, then cover and simmer for 20 minutes, stirring occasionally, until the sauce has thickened and the beef is thoroughly cooked.

3. Just before serving, heat a large dry frying pan until hot, and lightly toast the tortillas for 1-2 minutes on each side. Let them cool slightly then cut into strips.

4. Spoon the chilli into bowls and serve with crème fraîche, a few sprigs of coriander and the toasted tortilla strips.

Chilli con Carne (Serves 4)

Ingredients

1 tbsp vegetable oil

2 onions, chopped

1 clove garlic, crushed

450g/1lb lean minced beef

salt & pepper

1-2 tsps hot chilli powder

3 tbsps tomato puree

2 x 400g/14 oz cans tomatoes

150 ml/1/2 pt strong beef stock

2 x 450g/1lb cans red kidney beans, rinsed and drained

parsley sprigs, to garnish

Directions

1. Heat oil in a large saucepan, add onion and garlic and fry until soft. Add mince and fry until browned.

2. Add seasoning and chilli powder or chillies. Stir in tomato puree, tomatoes and stock. Bring to the boil, cover ana simmer for 45 minutes. Add kidney beans, cover and simmer for a further 15 minutes. Serve chilli on a bed of rice, garnished with parsley.

Chili Con Carne Nachos (Serves 4)

Ingredients

500g/1 lb 2oz lean minced beef

2 tbsps oil

2-3 red chilies, finely chopped

4 cloves garlic, crushed

2 medium onions, roughly chopped

2 tbsps coriander, stems chopped and leaves reserved

1 tbsp hot chilli powder

bayleaf

2 tsps ground cumin

2 tsps ground cinnamon

500ml/2 1/4 cups beef stock

3 tbsps tomato puree

2 x 420g/17oz cans red kidney beans, drained and rinsed

salt & freshly ground black pepper

Directions

1. Heat the oil in a large saucepan and fry the chilli, garlic and onions until soft.

2. Add the meat, coriander stems, chilli powder, bayleaf, cumin and cinnamon. Stir to combine and cook until the meat has browned. Add the stock and tomato puree and simmer for 20 minutes.

4. Add the kidney beans and simmer for a further 10 minutes, add seasoning to taste.

5. Sprinkle with the fresh coriander leaves. Serve with tortilla chips.

Chilli Stuffed Peppers (Serves 4)
Ingredients

4 green peppers, tops reserved and deseeded

Ingredients - for the filling

350g/12oz minced beef
1 onion, chopped
1 clove garlic, crushed
1 tbsp oil
100g/4oz mushrooms, sliced
2 tsps chilli powder
1 tbsp tomato puree
150ml/1/4 pint beef stock
425g/15oz can kidney beans
salt & pepper

Directions

1. Blanch the peppers in boiling salted water for 1 - 2 minutes and drain. Place in an ovenproof dish.

2. Fry the onion, garlic and minced beef in the oil until browned. Stir in the mushrooms, chilli powder, tomato puree, stock and seasoning and simmer gently for 10 minutes.

3. Drain the kidney beans and add to the meat. Fill the peppers with the chilli mixture, cover the dish and bake in a moderate oven for 30 minutes.

Mexican Beef (Serves 4)

Ingredients

500g/1lb minced beef

1-2 tbsps vegetable oil

1 small onion, finely chopped

1-2 tbsps chilli seasoning

2 tbsps quick-cooking porridge oats

300ml/1/2 pint beef stock

1 tbsp tomato puree

pinch of freshly grated nutmeg

salt & freshly ground black pepper

350g/12oz can sweetcorn with sweet peppers, drained

1 large or 2 medium avocados

1 tbsp lemon juice

100g/4oz Cheddar cheese, cut into 2.5cm (1 inch) cubes

Directions

1. Heat 1 tablespoon oil in a heavy-based saucepan. Add the beef and fry over moderate heat for 3 minutes, stirring constantly until all the beef has browned, breaking up any lumps with a wooden spoon.

2. Remove the beef with a slotted spoon. Add the onion to the pan and fry for 5 minutes until soft and lightly coloured, adding a further tablespoon oil if necessary, to prevent over-browning.

3. Return the beef to the pan, stir in 3 teaspoons chilli seasoning, then the oats, stock, tomato puree, nutmeg, salt to taste and add a light sprinkling of pepper.

4. Bring to the boil, stirring, then reduce the heat, cover and simmer gently for 40-45 minutes or until the oats are soft and the meat cooked.

5. Stir the drained sweetcorn and peppers into the beef mixture and continue to cook, uncovered, for 5 minutes until most of the excess liquid has evaporated. Taste and adjust seasoning, adding more chilli if a slightly hotter flavour is liked.

6. Just before serving, cut the avocado in half lengthways and discard the stone. Cut into quarters lengthways and peel away the skin, then cut the flesh into neat thin slices lengthways. Brush with the lemon juice to prevent discoloration.

7. Stir the cheese into the beef until just beginning to melt, then spoon the mixture into a warmed serving dish and arrange the avocado slices around the edge. Serve at once

Mexican Beefburgers with Tortillas and Avocado Salsa (Serves 4)

Ingredients - for the burgers

500g/1 lb pack lean steak mince
3 shallots or small onions, chopped
2 cloves garlic, finely chopped
2 fresh red or green chillies, deseeded and finely chopped
1 tsp paprika
chilli powder to taste
1/4 tsp ground cumin
2 tbsps chopped fresh coriander
1 tsp salt
freshly ground black pepper

Mexican Beefburgers with Tortillas and Avocado Salsa/Cont.

Ingredients - for the salsa

1 large avocado, stoned, peeled and chopped
250g/10oz cherry tomatoes, chopped
1 small red onion, finely chopped
2 fresh green chillies, deseeded and finely chopped
ground cumin and sugar to taste
2 tsps chopped fresh coriander
3 tsps olive oil
1 lime

Ingredients - for the tortillas

4 soft wheat tortillas
soured cream
shredded lettuce
cucumber (sliced)

Directions

1. Place the mince and all the burger ingredients, including the fresh coriander into a large bowl and mix together very well with your hands. Season with the salt and plenty of pepper, then mix again. Form into four large or eight medium burgers. Set aside.

2. To make the salsa, mix together the avocado, tomatoes, onion and chillies. Add grated lime zest and the juice of half the lime. Season with more lime juice and/or salt, cumin and sugar to taste. Stir in the chopped coriander and 1-2 tbsp olive oil. Set aside.

3. Brush the burgers with the remaining oil on both sides and either grill or fry in a non-stick pan over a medium-high heat for 4-5 minutes each side for the large burgers or 3-4 minutes each side for the smaller ones. They should be well-browned on the outside and cooked but still juicy on the inside, with no trace of pink remaining.

4. Place everything on the table and let each person fill their own tortilla with the burgers, salsa, soured cream, lettuce and cucumber to taste.

Mexican Jalapeno & Lime Burgers (Serves 4)

Ingredients

250g/10oz lean mince
zest and juice of a lime
1 small onoin, finely chopped
25g/1oz fresh breadcrumbs
1 Jalapeno pepper, deseeded & chopped
50g/2oz finely diced Monterey Jack cheese

Ingredients - for the guacamole

3 large ripe avocadoes, peeled and chopped
2 tbsps lemon juice
salt & pepper
1 tomato, coarsely chopped
2 spring onions, finely chopped

Ingredients - for the tomato salsa

400g/14oz tin tomatoes, drained and chopped
half a large onion, peeled and finely chopped
1 garlic clove, peeled and crushed
1 tbsp mixed herbs
1 tbsp tomato purée
1 tbsp olive oil
chilli powder, to taste

Ingredients - to serve

2 ciabattas, halved
4 tbsps of sour cream
1 lime quartered, for
garnish

Directions

1. In a large bowl mix
together all of the
ingredients until well
blended. Shape into four
burger patties with your hands.

Mexican Jalapeno & Lime Burgers/Cont.

2. Heat a little of the olive oil in a large non-stick frying pan and fry the burgers. Turn them once only, cooking for about 5-6 minutes each side.

3. Meanwhile, mash or process avocadoes with lemon juice until smooth. Season with salt and pepper and stir through chopped tomato and spring onions.

4. To make the salsa pour the tomatoes into a large mixing bowl, adding the onion, garlic, herbs, tomato purée and olive oil. Mix thoroughly and add the chilli powder to taste.

5. When the burgers are cooked, place each burger on a quarter of the ciabatta and serve piled with guacamole, salsa and sour cream and a lime quarter.

Mexican Minced Beef & Guacamole (Serves 4)

Ingredients

500g/1 lb 2oz lean beef mince
1 tbsp oil
1 onion, coarsely chopped
1 garlic clove, crushed
2 tsps ground cumin
2 tsps paprika
1/2 tsp cayenne pepper
140g/1/2 cup tomato paste
250ml/1 cup water or stock
pinch of sugar
salt
200g grated Cheddar cheese
toasted tortilla and sour cream, to serve

Ingredients - for the guacamole

3 large ripe avocadoes, peeled and chopped
2 tbsps lemon juice
salt & pepper
1 tomato, coarsely chopped
2 spring onions, finely chopped

Directions

1. Heat oil in a large pan over medium high heat; add onion and garlic and cook, stirring frequently for 2-3 minutes or until softened. Add mince in small batches and cook until browned and crumbly. Stir in spices and cook until spices are fragrant.

2. Add tomato paste into mince and mix well. Add water or stock and bring to the boil; reduce heat and simmer for 10-15 minutes. The mince should be tender and the sauce thickened. Season to taste with sugar and salt.

3. Meanwhile, mash or process avocadoes with lemon juice until smooth. Season with salt and pepper and stir through chopped tomato and green onions.

4. Spoon mince mixture into a serving dish then top with the guacamole mixture and grated cheese. Serve immediately with toasted tortillas and spoonful of sour cream.

Mexican Minced Beef & Spicy Polenta Cobbler (Serves 8)

Ingredients

8 tbsps sunflower oil

4 medium onions, finely chopped

8 garlic cloves, crushed

1 1/2 tsps crushed dried chillies

4 tsps freshly ground cumin seeds

1 tsp cayenne pepper

1kg/2 lbs 3oz lean minced beef

6 tbsps tomato purée

1 tbsp light muscovado sugar

2 tsps dried oregano

600ml/2 1/2 cups beef stock, hot

400g/16oz can chopped tomatoes

4 roasted red peppers from a jar, drained

2 x 400g/16oz cans red kidney beans in water, rinsed and drained

For the spicy polenta cobbler

400g/16oz plain flour

2 tbsps baking powder

2 tbsps soft brown sugar

1/2 tsp salt

1/2 tsp crushed dried chillies

175g/7oz polenta

125g/5oz Cheddar, finely grated

2 medium eggs

350ml/1 1/2 cups milk

4 tbsps sunflower oil

50g/2oz butter, melted

Directions

1. Heat the oil in a large pan, add the onions and garlic and cook for 10 minutes, until lightly browned. Add the chillies, cumin and cayenne and fry for 2-3 minutes.

2. Add the beef and cook over a high heat, breaking up with a wooden spoon as it browns. Add the purée, sugar, oregano, beef stock and tomatoes, bring to the boil, then simmer for 25 minutes, until reduced and thickened.

3. Finely chop the peppers and stir into the meat with the kidney beans. Season, then spoon into two large shallow, oval ovenproof dishes.

4. To make the cobbler, sift the flour, baking powder, sugar and salt into a large mixing bowl and stir in the chillies, polenta and 100g of grated cheese.

5. Beat the eggs, milk, oil and melted butter together and stir into the dry ingredients. Drop 8 spoonfuls of the mixture around the edge of each dish, about 2.5cm apart, and sprinkle with the remaining grated cheese.

6. To cook, preheat the oven to 220C/425°F/Gas mark 7. Bake for 20 minutes until bubbling and the topping is puffed up and golden.

Spiced Burrito Casserole (Serves 4)
Ingredients

700g/1 1/2 lb minced beef
1 large onion, peeled and diced
extra virgin olive oil
1 jar chunky salsa
2 tsps ground cumin
2 tsps chili powder
1/2 tsp minced garlic
50g/2oz green chilies, chopped
1 x 400g/16oz tin refried beans
1 pack whole-wheat tortillas
200g/8oz grated cheese

Directions

1. Pre-heat oven to 190°C/375°F/Gas mark 5. Sauté the mince and onions in extra virgin olive oil until meat is browned and onions are soft. Drain in a colander to remove excess fat.

2. Return meat and onions to the skillet and add garlic, cumin, chili powder, green chilies and salsa. Simmer for 15-20 minutes on medium heat. Lightly grease a 9 X 13-inch casserole dish with cooking spray, butter or oil.

3. Cut the tortillas in half. Place a layer of tortillas in the dish. Spread with half of the refried beans. Top with some of the meat mixture and some of the cheese.

Spiced Burrito Casserole/Cont.

4. Repeat until all ingredients are used, ending with a layer of cheese and bake for 20-25 minutes or until the cheese is bubbly.

Spiced Lamb Quesadillas (Serves 4)

Ingredients

450g/1 lb lean lamb mince

1 tsps ground coriander

1 tsps ground cumin

50g/2oz baby spinach leaves

2 tbsps freshly chopped flat-leaf parsley

8 flour tortillas

100g/4oz Feta cheese, crumbled

2 tbsps olive oil

salt & freshly milled black pepper

Ingredients for the Apple and Mint Salsa

1-2 large green apples, cored and diced

handful freshly chopped mint

1 tbsp of olive or groundnut oil

1 tbsp lime or lemon juice

1-2 tsps runny honey

Directions

1. Preheat the oven to 220°C/425°F/Gas mark 7. Heat a large shallow, non-stick frying pan and dry fry the mince with the spices and seasoning for 8-10 minutes. Remove from the heat and stir through the spinach and parsley.

2. Place 4 tortillas on a chopping board and spread evenly with the cheese then the lamb mixture. Sandwich together with the remaining tortillas, transfer to a non-stick baking sheet and brush with the oil.

3. Cook in the oven for 8-10 minutes until the tortillas are crispy and the lamb is cooked through.

4. Meanwhile prepare the salsa; in a small bowl mix all the ingredients together and set aside.

5. Slice each quesadilla in half and serve immediately with the apple and mint salsa and a green salad.

Tacos (Serves 4)

Ingredients

225g/8oz minced beef
1 small onion, chopped
1 tbsp raisins
1 tbsp pine nuts
1 tbsp sweetcorn
2 tsps chilli powder
120g/4oz canned tomatoes
salt & pepper
8 taco shells

Ingredients - toppings

120g/4oz grated cheese
140ml/1/4 pint sour cream
4 tomatoes, chopped
1/2 head lettuce, shredded
1 chopped avocado

Tacos/Cont.

Directions

1. Put the beef and onion into a 1 litre/2-pint casserole dish on the hob of the cooker. Break the meat up well with a fork.

2. Cover and cook for 4 minutes on high, stirring occasionally to break into small pieces.

3. Drain any fat from the meat and add the raisins, nuts, sweetcorn, chilli powder and tomatoes.

4. Cover and cook on a medium heat for 8 minutes. Adjust seasoning. Spoon into the taco shells and serve with the various toppings.

Beef Samosa (Makes 24)

Ingredients

500g/1 lb 2oz minced beef

1 onion

2 cloves garlic

1/2 tsp chili powder

1 tsp ground tumeric

1 tsp ground corriander

2 tsps fresh ginger

50 ml chopped mint

juice of 1 lemon

2 tbsps vegetable oil

salt & pepper, to taste

3 sheets of filo pastry or puff pastry

For samosas you want to fry, use filo pastry and for samosas you want to cook in the oven use puff pastry.

Directions

1. Heat the oil in a frying pan, add the onion and garlic mix in the spices and seasoning and fry until soft. Add the mince, stirring until cooked. Remove from heat and stir in the mint and lemon juice.

2. Divide the pastry into 12 equal pieces. Roll each piece into a ball and roll out into a circle of 15 cm. Divide this circle into two equal pieces with a knife.

3. Brush each edge with a little water and form a cone shape around your fingers, sealing the dampened edge.

4. Fill the cases with a tablespoon of your chosen mixture and press the two dampened edges together to seal the top of the cone. Deep fry the samosas in hot oil until crisp and brown take out and drain on a paper towel.

5. Alternatively, if you are baking the samosas bake in a preheated oven, 220°C/425°F/Gas mark 7, for 20-25 minutes until pastry is golden.

Keema Curry (Serves 4)

Ingredients

750g/1 lb 9oz minced beef
1 medium-sized onion, peeled and finely chopped
1 garlic clove, crushed with 1/2 tsp spoon salt
2 tsps spoons ground ginger
1 tbsp garam masala or curry powder
1/2 tsp spoon chilli powder
6 tomatoes, skinned, seeded and chopped
2 tbsps tomato puree
150 - 300ml/1/4 - 1/2 pint beef stock
2 x 140g/5oz cartons natural unsweetened yogurt
cooking oil for frying

Directions

1. Heat 2 spoons of oil in a large frying pan. Add the onion, garlic and ginger and fry until golden. Stir in the minced beef, garam masala or curry powder and chilli powder and fry until the meat is browned, stirring constantly.

2. Add the tomatoes, tomato puree, 150 ml (1/4 pint) of the stock and half the yogurt and mix well.

3. Cover and simmer gently for about 30 minutes or until the beef is cooked, adding more stock if the mixture becomes dry. Taste for seasoning, stir in the remaining yogurt and transfer to a hot serving platter.

Keema Lamb (Serves 4)

Ingredients

500g/1lb pack lamb mince
1 onion, finely chopped
2 garlic cloves, finely chopped
4 tomatoes, finely chopped
2 tbsps of your favourite curry paste
200ml/1 cup coconut milk

Directions

1. Heat a deep, wide frying pan. Add the mince, onion and garlic and fry for 5 minutes. Stir in the tomatoes, curry paste and coconut milk. Simmer for 30 minutes.

2. Serve with steamed rice and garnish with fresh coriander.

If freezing: Cool, then freeze in a large freezer-proof container. Cover and freeze for up to 3 months. Defrost at room temperature, then heat thoroughly.

Keema Naan (Serves 4)

Ingredients

225g/1/2 lb lamb mince
1 tbsp mild curry powder
2 tbsps tomato purée
2 plain naan
2 tbsps chopped fresh coriander

Directions

1. Fry the mince in a nonstick pan, without any oil, until browned. Stir in the curry powder, cook for 2 minutes, stirring, add the tomato purée and cook for 3 to 4 minutes.

2. Meanwhile, warm the naan, cut in half widthways, then slice open to make a pocket.

3. Mix coriander into mince and divide mixture between naans, gently pressing them flat. Sprinkle with water and grill for 2 minutes.

Lamb Samosa (Makes 24)

Ingredients

500g/1 lb 2oz minced lamb
1 onion
2 cloves of garlic crushed
1 tsp curry powder
1/2 tsp chilli powder
1 tsp ground tumeric
1/2 tsp ground roasted cumin seeds
1 chilli, deseed and diced
1 tsp chopped corriander--
1/2 tsp fresh grated ginger
salt & pepper
juice of half a lemon
3 sheets of filo pastry or puff pastry
For samosas you want to fry, use filo pastry and for samosas you want to cook in the oven use puff pastry.

Directions

1. Heat the oil in a frying pan, add the onion and garlic mix in the spices and seasoning and fry until soft. Add the mince, stirring until cooked. Remove from heat and stir in the mint and lemon juice.

2. Divide the pastry into 12 equal pieces. Roll each piece into a ball and roll out into a circle of 15 cm. Divide this circle into two equal pieces with a knife.

3. Brush each edge with a little water and form a cone shape around your fingers, sealing the dampened edge.

4. Fill the cases with a tablespoon of your chosen mixture and press the two dampened edges together to seal the top of the cone. Deep fry the samosas in hot oil until crisp and brown take out and drain on a paper towel.

5. Alternatively, if you are baking the samosas bake in a preheated oven, 220°C/425°F/Gas mark 7, for 20-25 minutes until pastry is golden.

Mongolian Beef (Serves 4)
Ingredients

600g/1 lb 5oz quality beef mince, ground beef
300g/11oz Chinese cabbage, finely shredded
2 tsps sea salt
2 tbsps vegetable oil
2 tbsps Chinese rice wine, shao hsing
2 tbsps hoisin sauce
1 tbsp oyster sauce
1 tsp malt vinegar
1/2 tsp sesame oil
80g/3oz carrots, peeled and finely sliced
220g/9oz red capsicum, seeded and finely sliced
50g/2oz spring onions, the white part finely sliced
spring onions, the green part for garnishing

Ingredients - for the marinade

2 tbsps Chinese rice wine, shao hsing or dry sherry
1 tbsp light soy sauce
1 tbsp cornflour
1 tbsp ginger, finely diced
4 cloves garlic, finely diced
1/2 tsp sesame oil

Directions

1. Mix together the marinade ingredients, combine with the beef and store covered for 30 minutes in the fridge.

Mongolian Beef/Cont.

2. Meanwhile mix together well the cabbage and salt. Let stand for 15 minutes then rinse under cold water and drain. Squeeze out excess liquid with your hands.

3. Heat the oil in a hot wok or heavy-based pan and stir-fry half the marinated beef for about 1 minute until it is just cooked through. Break up any lumps with a spoon. Remove from the wok with a slotted spoon and set aside.

4. Stir in remaining beef, adding a little more oil if necessary, and cook, stirring for 40 seconds.

5. Return reserved beef to the wok with wine or sherry, hoisin sauce, oyster sauce, vinegar and sesame oil and stir-fry for about 30 seconds.

6. Add cabbage, carrots and capsicum and stir-fry for a further minute. Stir spring onions and remove from the heat.

7. Sprinkle the dish with the green parts of the spring onions and serve immediatly with rice and some sliced chillies on the side.

Pork Noodles (Serves 4)

Ingredients

500g/1 lb 2oz pork mince
2 tbsps oyster sauce
1 tbsp sweet chilli sauce
2 tbsps soy sauce
1/2 cucumber
2 tbsps vegetable oil
3cm fresh ginger, grated
3 spring onions, finely chopped
1 tbsp cornflour
1 tbsp chinese rice wine
600g/1 lb 5oz egg noodles

Directions

1. Stir together the oyster, sweet chilli and soy sauces with 125ml water. Using a potato peeler, shave the cucumber lengthwise, either side of the central seeds, into thin ribbons.

2. Heat a wok. Add the oil, followed by the ginger and spring onions. Stir-fry over a high heat for 30 seconds. Add the pork and stir-fry for 4–6 minutes until browned. Add the sauce mixture and simmer for 4 minutes. Mix the cornflour with the rice wine and add to the meat, stirring. Simmer until the sauce thickens.

3. Put the noodles in a large bowl and pour over a kettleful of boiling water. Allow them to soften for 4 minutes then drain well. Divide the noodles between 4 warmed bowls. Top with the spicy mince and a few furls of cucumber.

Quick Beef Curry (Serves 4)

Ingredients

500g/1 lb lean minced beef
1 large onion, chopped
1 clove garlic, crushed (optional)
1 tbsp curry powder
1/4 tsp ground ginger
1/4 tsp ground cumin
1 dessert apple, peeled and grated
2 tbsps sultanas or seedless raisins
300g/10oz can condensed beef consomme
salt & freshly ground black pepper
100g/4 oz mushrooms, quartered

Directions

1 Place the beef, onion and garlic in a saucepan and fry over moderate heat until the beef is well browned, stirring constantly to break up lumps.

2 Stir in the spices and cook for 2 minutes, then stir in the apple,sultanas and the beef consomme. Season to taste with salt and pepper.

3 Bring to the boil, then simmer gently for 5 minutes.

4 Stir in the mushrooms and simmer a further 10 minutes. Taste and adjust seasoning. Serve at once.

My Recipe

Ingredients:

Preparation:

My Recipe

Ingredients:

Preparation:

My Recipe

Ingredients:

Preparation:

My Recipe

Ingredients:

Preparation:

My Recipe

Ingredients:

Preparation:

My Recipe

Ingredients:

Preparation:

My Recipe

Ingredients:

Preparation:

My Recipe

Ingredients:

Preparation:

My Recipe

Ingredients:

Preparation:

My Recipe

Ingredients:

Preparation:

INDEX

The recipes contained in this book are passed on in good faith but the publisher cannot be held responsible for any adverse results. Please be aware that certain recipes may contain nuts. The recipes use both metric and imperial measurements, and the reader should not mix metric and imperial measurements. Spoon measurements are level, teaspoons are assumed to be 5ml, tablespoons 15ml. For other measurements, see chart below. Times given are for guidance only, as preparation techniques may vary and can lead to different cooking times.

Spoons to millilitres

1/2 teaspoon	2.5 ml	1 Tablespoon	15 ml
1 teaspoon	5 ml	2 Tablespoons	30 ml
1-1 1/2 teaspoons	7.5 ml	3 Tablespoons	45 ml
2 teaspoons	10 ml	4 Tablespoons	60 ml

Grams to ounces

10g	0.25oz	225g	8oz
15g	0.38oz	250g	9oz
25g	1oz	275g	10oz
50g	2oz	300g	11oz
75g	3oz	350g	12oz
110g	4oz	375g	13oz
150g	5oz	400g	14oz
175g	6oz	425g	15oz
200g	7oz	450g	16oz

Metric to cups

Description		
Flour etc	115g	1 cup
Clear honey etc	350g	1 cup
Liquids etc	225ml	1 cup

Liquid measures

5fl oz	1/4 pint	150 ml
7.5fl oz		215 ml
10fl oz	1/2 pint	275 ml
15fl oz		425 ml
20fl oz	1 pint	570 ml
35fl oz		1 litre

Oven Temperatures

Gas mark	°F	°C
1	275°F	140°C
2	300°F	150°C
3	325°F	170°C
4	350°F	180°C
5	375°F	190°C
6	400°F	200°C
7	425°F	220°C
8	450°F	230°C
9	475°F	240°C

Food Safety Tips

Safe steps in food handling, cooking, and storage are essential to avoiding food borne illness. Follow these food safety guidelines.

Safe Shopping Buy cold food last; get it home fast.

Never choose packages which are torn or leaking.

Don't buy foods past "sell-by" or expiration dates.

Put raw meat and poultry in a plastic bag so juices won't cross-contaminate cooked foods or those eaten raw, such as vegetables or fruit.

Place refrigerated or frozen items in the shopping cart last, right before heading for the checkout counter.

Safe Storage of Foods Keep it safe; refrigerate.

Unload perishables from the car first and immediately refrigerate them.

Place securely wrapped packages of raw meat, poultry, or fish in the meat drawer or coldest section of your refrigerator.

Check the temperature of your unit with an appliance thermometer. To slow bacterial growth, the refrigerator should be at 40° F; the freezer, 0° F.

Cook or freeze fresh poultry, fish and meat within 3 to 5 days.

Safe Food Preparation Keep everything clean!

Hands should be washed thoroughly after using the bathroom and before preparing or eating food.
Wash hands before and after handling raw meat and poultry.
Sanitize cutting boards, kitchen towels and cloths regularly.
Don't cross-contaminate. Keep raw meat, poultry, fish, and their juices away from other food. After cutting raw meats, wash hands, cutting board, knife, and counter tops with hot, soapy water.
Marinate meat and poultry in a covered dish in the refrigerator.
Always wash fresh fruits and vegetables under cool running tap water before eating. This removes any lingering dirt while also removing or reducing any bacteria or other substances.
Certain hearty vegetables, such as potatoes and carrots. can be scrubbed with a produce brush if consumers plan to eat the fiber and nutrient-rich skin.
When preparing fruits and vegetables, cut away bruised or damaged areas.

Thaw Food Safely

Refrigerator: Allow slow, safe thawing. Make sure thawing juices do not drip on other foods.
Cold Water: For faster thawing, place food in a leak-proof plastic bag and submerge in cold tap water.
Microwave: Cook meat and poultry immediately after microwave thawing.

Safe Cooking

Cook mince to 160° F; ground poultry to 165° F. Beef, veal and lamb steaks, roasts, and chops may be cooked to 145° F; all cuts of fresh pork, 160° F. Whole poultry should reach 180° F in the thigh; breasts, 170° F.

Serving Food Safely

Never leave it out over 2 hours. (1 hour in temperature above 90 °F) Bacteria that cause food borne illness grow rapidly at room temperature.

Keep hot food hot! Cold food cold!

When serving food at a buffet, keep hot food over a heat source and keep cold food on ice. Keep platters of food refrigerated until time to serve or heat them.
Carry perishable picnic food in a cooler with a cold pack or ice. Set the cooler in the shade and open the lid as little as possible.

Handling Leftovers Safely

Divide foods into shallow containers for rapid cooling. Put food directly in the refrigerator or freezer.
Cut turkey off the bone and refrigerate. Slice breast meat; legs and wings may be left whole.
Use cooked leftovers within 4 days.
Cut or cooked produce items. such as baked potatoes or vegetable casseroles, should never be left out or held at room temperature for an extended time period.